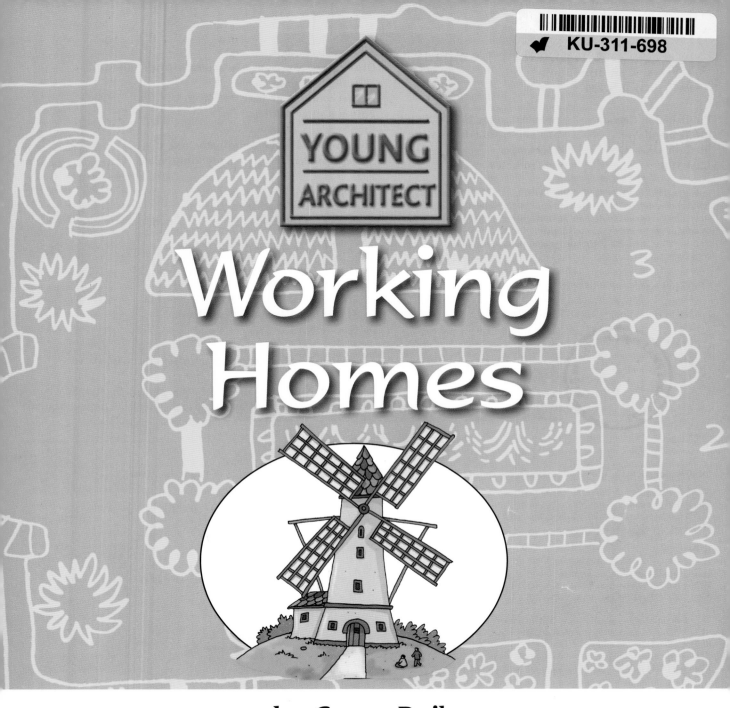

YOUNG ARCHITECT

Working Homes

by Gerry Bailey

Illustrated by Moreno Chiacchiera, Michelle Todd, and Joelle Dreidemy

Crabtree Publishing Company

Crabtree Publishing Company
www.crabtreebooks.com
1-800-387-7650

Published in Canada
616 Welland Ave.
St. Catharines, ON
L2M 5V6

Published in the United States
PMB 59051, 350 Fifth Ave.
59th Floor,
New York, NY

Printed in Hong Kong/092013/BK20130703

Author: Gerry Bailey
Illustrators: Moreno Chiacchiera, Michelle Todd,
  Joelle Dreidemy
Project coordinator: Kelly McNiven
Editor: Kathy Middleton
Proofreader: Crystal Sikkens
**Print and Production coordinator and
  Prepress technician:** Margaret Amy Salter

Photographs:
Pg 4	Thinkstock.com
Pg 9	(l) (m) Elena Elisseeva; (r) margouillat photo
Pg 12	Kamira
Pg 14/15	f9photos
Pg 15	Alvov
Pg 19	Paul Almasy / CORBIS
Pg 21	(t) cozyta; (b) Hung Chung Chih
Pg 24/25	age fotostock / SuperStock
Pg 28	NASA

All images are Shutterstock.com unless otherwise stated.

Every attempt has been made to clear copyright. Should there be any
inadvertent omission, please apply to the publisher for rectification.

Library and Archives Canada Cataloguing in Publication

Bailey, Gerry, author
    Working homes / by Gerry Bailey ; illustrated by Moreno Chiacchiera,
Michelle Todd and Joelle Dreidemy.

(Young architect)
Includes index.
Issued in print and electronic formats.
ISBN 978-0-7787-0290-0 (bound).--ISBN 978-0-7787-0300-6 (pbk.).--
ISBN 978-1-4271-1279-8 (pdf).--ISBN 978-1-4271-1275-0 (html)

    1. Buildings--Juvenile literature. 2. Dwellings--Juvenile literature.
I. Chiacchiera, Moreno, illustrator II. Todd, Michelle, 1978-, illustrator
III. Dreidemy, Joelle, illustrator IV. Title.

TH149.B33 2013   j728   C2013-904067-6
                                      C2013-904068-4

Library of Congress Cataloging-in-Publication Data

Bailey, Gerry.
 Working homes / Written by Gerry Bailey ; Illustrated by Moreno Chiacchiera,
Michelle Todd, and Joelle Dreidemy.
    pages cm. -- (Young architect)
 Includes index.
 ISBN 978-0-7787-0290-0 (reinforced library binding) -- ISBN 978-0-7787-0300-6 (pbk.) --
ISBN 978-1-4271-1279-8 (electronic pdf) -- ISBN 978-1-4271-1275-0 (electronic html)
 1. Buildings--Juvenile literature. 2. Dwellings--Juvenile literature. I. Chiacchiera,
Moreno, illustrator. II. Title.

TH149.B33 2013
728--dc23
                    2013023897

Contents

Introduction

Imagine living and working in the same building! Many people have to travel to work each day, but in a windmill, all you would have to do is just climb some stairs. And you would have to climb even more stairs if you lived and worked in a lighthouse. Many jobs can be done from home. In the past, workers such as blacksmiths would carry out their work on the ground floor and live upstairs. Others, like the **bellringer**, sometimes stayed in the bell tower to be close to the bell when it had to be rung. Let's find out about these working homes.

Living in a windmill

The sails of a windmill will turn all night and day as long as the wind is blowing. The turning sails move the machinery inside the mill. If the wind is blowing, the mill is working, and the miller works, too! That's why the mill is also the miller's home.

Windmills, which use the power of the wind to grind wheat into flour, are found all over the world. They are usually built on flat countryside that does not have fast-running rivers to provide the power.

Today, mills use newer technology, but many old windmills still work, and many are still used as homes.

A material called sailcloth covers the blades of the windmill and catches the wind.

The rooms

The wheat to be ground into flour is kept in the grain store.

The sacks of grain are raised to the grinding stones using a sack hoist.

An axle joins the sails to a series of gears.

As the sails turn, they turn the shaft.

The shaft then turns the millstone.

The millstone grinds the grain into flour.

The flour drops down a funnel and is collected for the bakery.

A brake can stop the sails from turning.

At the bottom is a living room and bedrooms for the miller and his family.

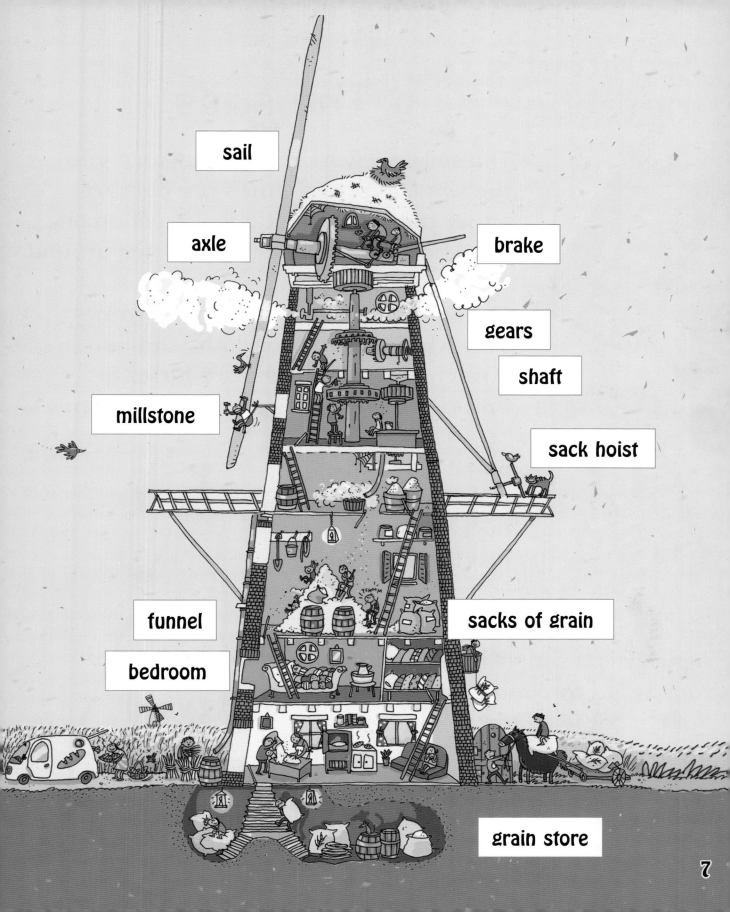

sail

axle

brake

gears

shaft

millstone

sack hoist

funnel

sacks of grain

bedroom

grain store

7

Architect's notebook

- The sails -

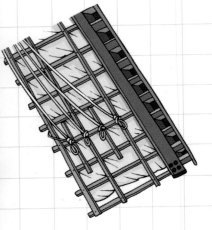

The sails will work only if they face into the wind. Many windmills are built so either the sails can change direction or the whole **structure** can be turned around.

The sails are usually four open frames over which canvas sailcloths can be stretched. These cloths are **furled** or unfurled using ropes attached to them.

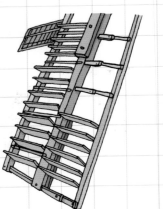

Some sails have **slats** that can be pulled open or closed just like shutters.

- The pulley -

A **pulley** is a simple machine in which a rope is fed through wheels with grooves. Pulleys are used to raise heavy sacks of grain up to the grinding floor. The more wheels and the longer the rope, the easier it is.

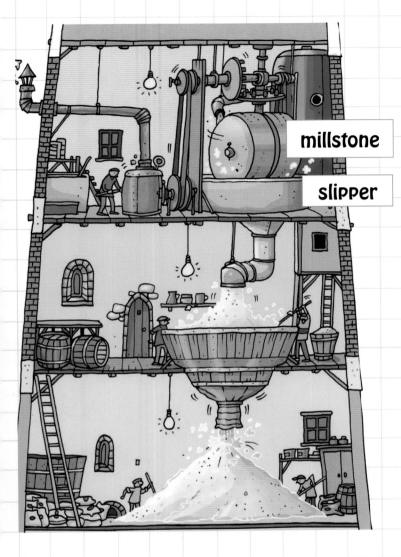

millstone

slipper

The sacks of grain are raised to the top floor using the sack hoist, or pulley.

Next, the grain is tipped into **slippers**. These are shallow troughs. They constantly vibrate, keeping the seeds spread out. They also make sure the grain falls under the millstones at a steady rate.

One millstone turns while the other remains still. The grain is crushed in the grooves cut into each stone.

As the wheat ripens, large grains appear and swell.

The grains are separated from the stalks.

The ground wheat is called flour. It is made into bread and cakes.

Under the waves

Some people live on top of the waves, others live underneath them. Sailors who work in submarines are called submariners, and they spend long periods of time living beneath the sea. A submariner can spend months without coming to the surface. Nuclear submarines have even sailed under the North Pole.

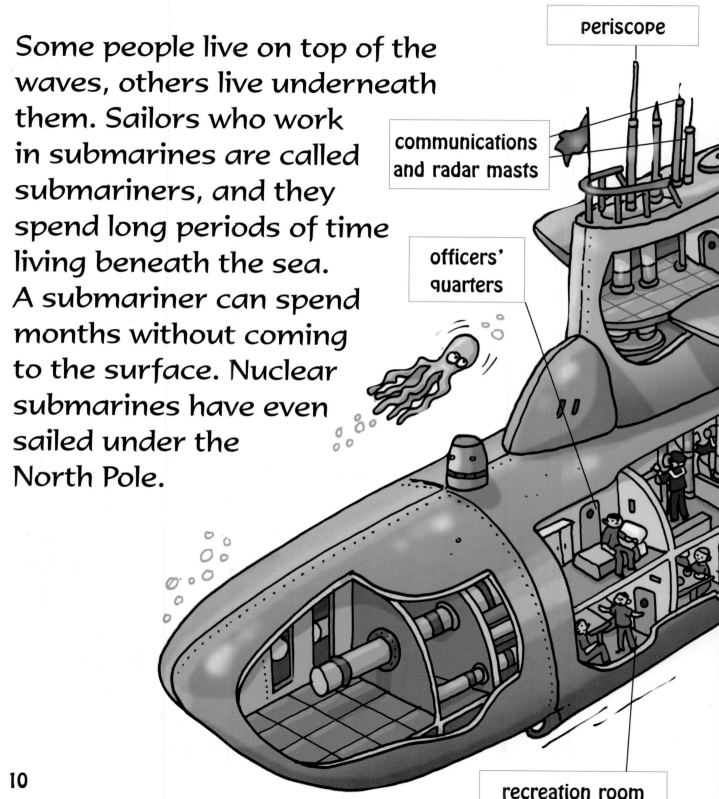

periscope

communications and radar masts

officers' quarters

recreation room

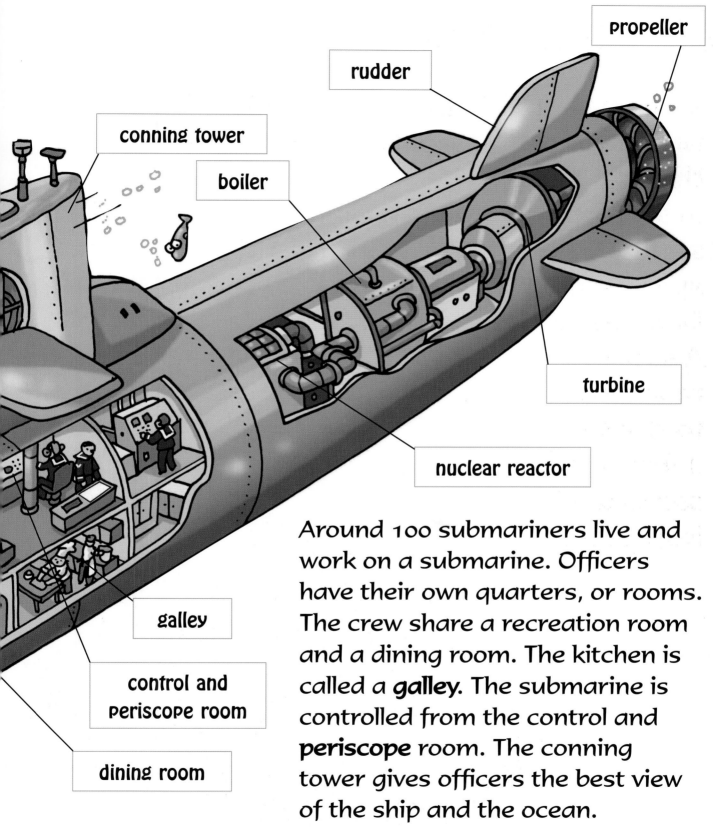

propeller

rudder

conning tower

boiler

turbine

nuclear reactor

galley

control and periscope room

dining room

Around 100 submariners live and work on a submarine. Officers have their own quarters, or rooms. The crew share a recreation room and a dining room. The kitchen is called a **galley**. The submarine is controlled from the control and **periscope** room. The conning tower gives officers the best view of the ship and the ocean.

High on the rocks

A lighthouse is a tower that warns ships of dangerous places or guides them to a place of safety. Its warning light is a powerful beam that can be seen far out to sea.

Sailors recognize the beam of each lighthouse by the way it flashes, by its color, or by the length of time between flashes.

The lighthouse may be built on a rock in the sea. In the past, the lighthouse keeper had a lonely job, especially during stormy weather when it was not possible to reach the shore to get supplies.

Today, most lighthouses are **automated** and do not require anyone to live there. The keeper only visits to check that everything is in working order.

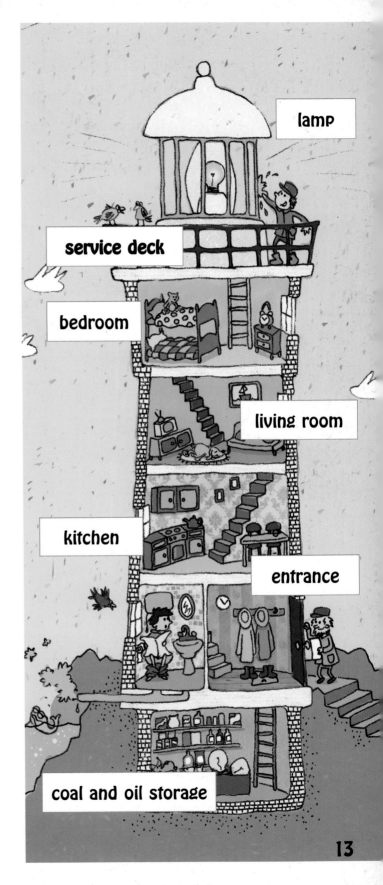

lamp

service deck

bedroom

living room

kitchen

entrance

coal and oil storage

13

Lights at the top

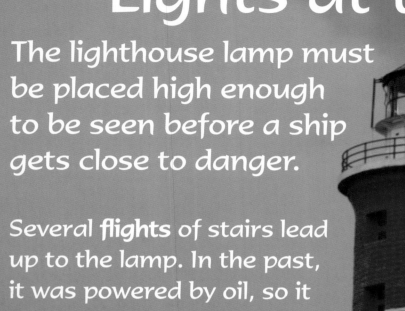

The lighthouse lamp must be placed high enough to be seen before a ship gets close to danger.

Several **flights** of stairs lead up to the lamp. In the past, it was powered by oil, so it had to be lit by hand each night. Glass lenses were placed around the light to **magnify** the beam and point its light in one direction.

Today, **strobe lights** are used. These are very powerful beams that flash on and off automatically.

From a ship, you do not see a continuous light. Instead you see a brighter light for short bursts. These flashes create a pattern of lights that are special to each lighthouse. For example, one lighthouse might flash for two seconds and then seven seconds, over and over again.

Some lighthouse lamps even include color flashes to warn of certain kinds of dangers.

The lighthouse keeper's daughter

Grace Darling had watched the storm rage all night from an upstairs window of the Longstone Lighthouse where she lived with her father.

But now, she could see the shape of a boat just off the shore. And, to her horror, she watched as it was swept against a rocky island and broken in half.

In their small row boat, Grace and her father started to row out in the rough waves. At the wreck, they were able to pull five people into the boat. While Grace took care of them at the lighthouse, her father and the rescued men went back again for the rest of the survivors. Today, Grace Darling is remembered as a brave **heroine**.

Over the shop

Some buildings where people live are actually designed as workplaces as well as homes. For example, the front room of a home might be a shop, not a living room.

Long ago, in Singapore, many Chinese shopkeepers lived in shophouses. Rows of shophouses often had a covered walkway in front to protect customers from the Sun or rain. Above the shop was the home of the shop owner and family.

The blacksmith

In North America, a blacksmith was a person who made items, such as horseshoes, out of metal for the early settlers. His place of work, or **forge**, was part of the home. In the forge there was a hearth, or furnace, for heating the metal and an anvil—a specially shaped iron workbench— for bending the metal into objects.

This blacksmith uses a hammer to shape a piece of metal on his **anvil**.

The bellringer

In the past, bells were rung to call people together or to warn them of danger. The **belfry** is the name of the room at the top of the tower where the huge bells hung. Some towers had a room where the bellringer could stay so they could ring the bells quickly when it was needed.

19

A Hakka village

For centuries, the Hakka people of China built large circular buildings known as **tulou**. Here, many families lived under the same roof, making the building like a village. A high wall runs around the structure to defend it from enemy tribes. For the same reason, there is only one entrance to the tulou and no windows at ground level.

Why are these buildings round? It may be because of **superstition**. In a round building there are no corners where a bad spirit can hide! Or they may have started out as round watchtowers, and then developed into homes.

At the center of the tulou is an **altar** and a place for worship. The center is ringed by homes, shops, stores, businesses, and services. Many families still live in tulou.

The streets run in circles
inside the tulou.

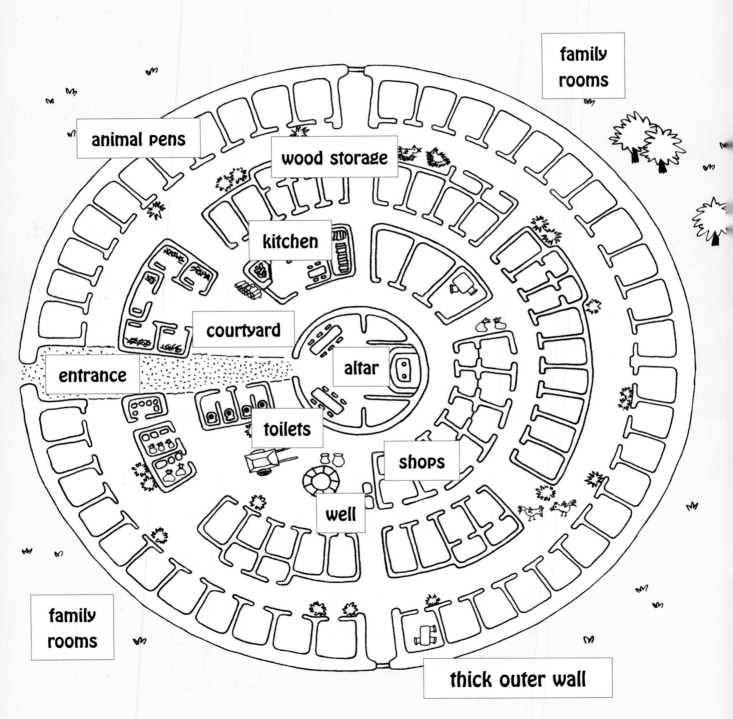

family rooms

animal pens

wood storage

kitchen

courtyard

altar

entrance

toilets

shops

well

family rooms

thick outer wall

Inside the Hakka tulou

Up to 250 small rooms look out on to the inner courtyard. The building can be three stories high.

A single family has two or three rooms on each floor.

The kitchen is shared by everyone. It has a large oven heated with firewood.

The meat and vegetables are prepared in the courtyard.

The altar where ancestors are honored is in the central building of the village.

The courtyard is used for drying clothes and rice, for village activities, and for children to play.

There are animal pens and a well for water in the courtyard, too.

On the ranch

Would you like to live on a large farm with a lot of animals and a lot of land? Some ranches, especially in the United States and Australia, can stretch over thousands of miles. Many thousands of sheep or cows graze on the land.

Some big ranches have more than 40 buildings. Many are made of wood from trees that have been chopped down to clear the land for farming.

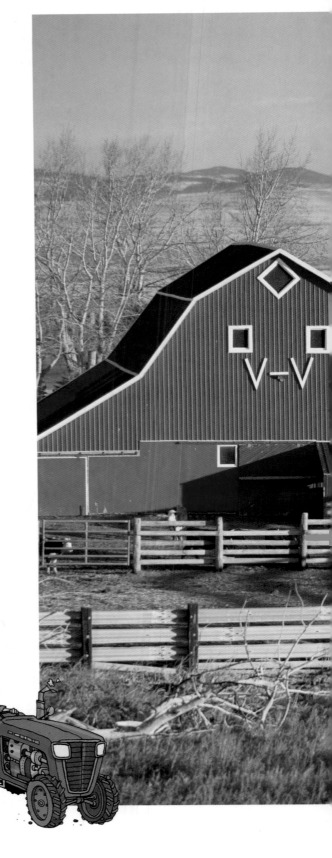

The ranch outbuildings

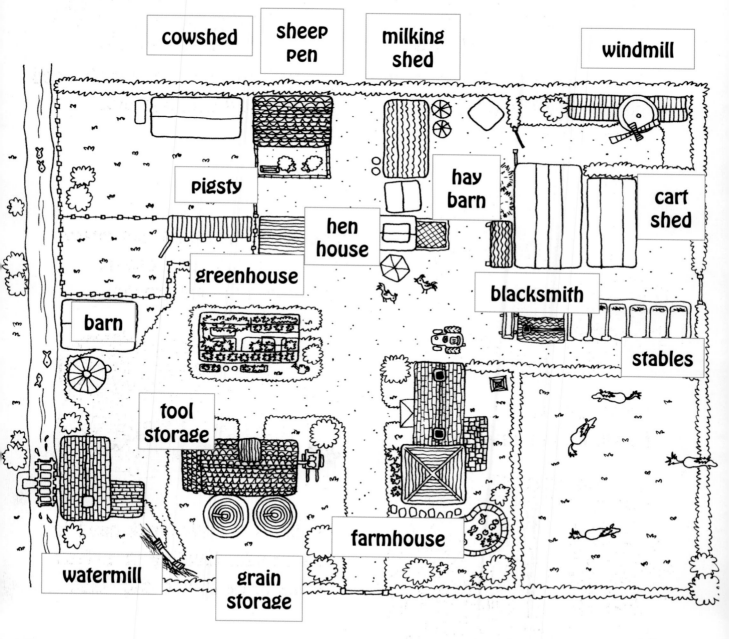

cowshed

sheep pen

milking shed

windmill

pigsty

hay barn

cart shed

hen house

greenhouse

blacksmith

barn

stables

tool storage

farmhouse

watermill

grain storage

Hens have a hen house, and pigs have a sty. All the other animals each need a dry home.

Farm machinery and tools need to be kept safe and dry.

On a ranch, it is important that every kind of animal has a pen, feeding area, and room to move around.

Crops and wood need to be stored in a dry place.

Animals that give milk need to be brought together in a clean place to be milked each day.

27

Working in space

Welcome to the International Space Station, the working home of up to six astronauts. Life in space means you are floating around with no **gravity**. The crew members are busy and work for 14 hours a day. Then they must exercise, eat, and sleep.

The space station travels so fast that it orbits Earth every 90 minutes—that's 16 times a day!

There is a special dining area with water, microwave ovens, and refrigerators, so you can eat normal foods, such as fruit, vegetables, and ice cream!

Each crew member has a private room, or galley. Without gravity, you must be anchored down in your bed so you don't float away.

You have to wear a special space suit on the journey, but once you are safely inside the space station, you can wear ordinary clothing. Of course, a special pressurized space suit is needed to go outside the space station so you are not hurt by space debris or burned by the hot Sun.

Exercise is important since muscles and bones grow weak in space. You must exercise on bikes, rowing machines, and other equipment for about two hours every day.

A simple task like brushing your teeth is a challenge. Water doesn't trickle away—it hangs in bubbles! Astronauts use one hose to shower, shampoo, and rinse off, then a second hose to suck off the dirty water.

Glossary

altar A raised platform used as a center for worship

anvil An iron workbench for shaping hot metal

automated Something that has been changed to operate itself or without a person controlling it

axle The center bar around which a wheel revolves

belfry A high room in a tower where a set of bells is hung

bellringer The worker who looked after the bells in a bell tower

flight A set of stairs from one floor to the other

forge The room in which a blacksmith works with a hot fire and tools

furled Rolled up or gathered

galley A small kitchen and dining area on a boat or aircraft

gravity The force that attracts objects and pulls them toward the surface of Earth

heroine A woman who is looked up to by others

magnify To make something look bigger than it is

periscope A long tube on top of a submarine that sticks out of the surface of the water. People can look through the periscope from inside the submarine to see things above the water.

pulley A device for lifting objects using a rope and grooved wheels

service deck The top story of a lighthouse, from which the light can be serviced or fixed

slat A kind of shutter in a windmill sail that can be opened or closed

slipper In a windmill, this is a vibrating trough that holds the grain

strobe light A strong beam of light that flashes on and off

structure Another name for the framework of a building

superstition A belief based on fear or lack of knowledge

tulou The enclosed, round village buildings of the Chinese Hakka people

Learning more

Books:

Build It: Invent New Structures and Contraptions. Tammy Enz. Capstone Press, 2012.
Readers are encouraged to use their imaginations to create amazing contraptions in this how-to book.

Look At That Building! A First Book of Structures. Scot Ritchie. Kids Can Press, 2011.
Five friends set out to build a doghouse and explore basic construction concepts including foundations, frames, and other building fundamentals.

Homes That Move. Nicola Barber. Crabtree Publishing, 2008.
This book explores the materials and features of homes that move, including houseboats and igloos.

Websites:

PBS's Building Big video and website:
www.pbs.org/wgbh/buildingbig/
This website includes activities as it explores bridges, skyscrapers, and more.

Archkidecture:
www.archkidecture.org/
This website gives a lot of basic information on architecture for kids.

The Great Buildings Collection:
www.greatbuildings.com/
Readers receive design and architectural information on a thousand buildings from around the world.

Structures Around the World: Activities for the Elementary Classroom:
www.exploratorium.edu/structures/
Readers learn all about structures through hands-on activities provided by the Exploratorium museum.

Try Engineering:
www.tryengineering.org/lesson.php
This website features lessons plans and activities that explore engineering principles.

Index